Breaking Every Demonic Spell

DELIVERANCE SERIES VOLUME 14

Bishop Climate Irungu

Contents

Balaam & Balak

"A people has come out of Egypt, they cover the face of the land and have settled next to me. Now come and put a curse on these people, because they are too powerful for me. Perhaps then I will be able to defeat them and drive them out of the land. For I know that whoever you bless is blessed, and whoever you curse is cursed." (Num 22:5-6)

"Balaam said, 'Build me seven altars here, and prepare seven bulls and seven rams for me.' Balak did as Balaam said, and the two of them offered a bull and a ram on each altar. Then Balaam said to Balak, 'Stay here beside your offering while I go aside. Perhaps the LORD will come to meet with me. Whatever he reveals to me I will tell you.' Then he went off to a barren height." (Num 23:1-3)

PART ONE

Breaking Every Demonic Spell

One of the things I know you've been wondering about is why every time you start something new, every time you get interested in a new project, every time an opportunity comes along, it is never able to take off; something is always hindering you. It almost makes you feel as though you can never have anything good in life because something always comes to try and snatch it from you. But it is because somebody had released a spell over your life to make sure you never succeed.

The Bible talks about a king named Balak in the

book of Numbers 22-23 who summoned one of the most powerful witch doctors in the land, Balaam, to be able to put a curse on the children of Israel.

Then the Israelites travelled to the plains of Moab and camped along the Jordan across from Jericho. Now Balak son of Zippor saw all that Israel had done to the Amorites, and Moab was terrified because there were so many people. Indeed, Moab was filled with dread because of the Israelites. The Moabites said to the elders of
Midian, "This horde is going to lick up everything around us, as an ox licks up the grass of the field." So Balak son of Zippor, who was king of Moab at that time, sent messengers to summon Balaam son of Beor, who was at Pethor, near the Euphrates River, in his native land. Balak said: "A people has come out of Egypt; they cover the face of the land and have settled next to me. Now come and put a curse on these people, because they are too powerful for me. Perhaps then I will be able to defeat them and drive them out of the land. For I know that whoever you bless is blessed, and whoever you curse is cursed."

(Num 22:1-6)

One of the things you're going to have to realize is that your life is not a secret. Even when you plan to do something, you are not the only one that knows. Because anytime God is about to do something great in your life, your enemies know that something is going on.

Moab was terrified for they had heard the stories about how Israel had destroyed other nations, and when they saw how big the Israelite army was they were filled with fear.

The people that are trying to fight you are so scared of you. They know that you are capable of great success and that is why they are trying everything in their power to destroy you.

The King of Moab said that "a people had come out of Egypt, they cover the face of the land, and have settled next to me."

When the children of Israel came out of Egypt it signified their deliverance. And the enemy knew it. He knew that this tribe was no longer the tribe that was enslaved to Pharaoh, no something was different. And it is the same thing with you. You are going through your deliverance and there is another power behind you that's why your enemies are so scared of you. Because they know that once you come out you are going to take over. You are going to recover all the years that the locusts have eaten.

As long as the children of Israel encamped against Moab, the king of Moab was agitated.

There is someone that has been agitated about you. Since you got that position at work, they have been agitated. Since you bought that new car, since that person got interested in you, someone has been agitated. Since the day you started looking good, somebody has been agitated. The day you decided to improve your life, somebody got agitated; someone is against your progress.

You are the only one in your family who chose to be somebody, because of that they shut your door. When they heard you were getting ready to go to another level, they shut your doors. But I came to let you know that every spell that has been released over your life, God is about to break its powers.

Whosoever has been agitated because you want to move forward, today they are going to die by fire!

As long as the children of Israel were not there King Balak was fine, but as soon as they were next to him he became agitated.

There is someone that never wants your children to talk to you. Anytime they do somebody gets agitated. But today that curse must be broken. Every barrier between you and your children must die by fire!

Verse 6 says,

Now come and put a curse on these people, because they are too powerful for me. Perhaps then I will be able to defeat them and drive them out of the land. For I know that whoever you bless is blessed, and whoever you curse is cursed."

Now why would Balak ask Balaam to put a curse on them so that he could defeat them? Because what you need to understand is that a curse is not just a five-letter word. No, it is an empowerment to fail.

So that no matter what they do they will fail. They will be too weak to stand against their enemies so their enemies will always prevail.

You wonder why in your finances nothing seems to be working. Because there is a curse that has been released over your life, something supernatural has been weakening your finances, something supernatural has been generating failure in your life, but today God is going to revoke every demonic force against you in Jesus name.

You are wondering what it is you are doing wrong, but there is NOTHING! You need to understand that your enemies are not fighting you physically; if they were then they would fail. They are using spiritual powers against you because they know you are stronger than them.

Balak asked Balaam to put a curse on them because they were too powerful for them. Your enemies have been putting curses on you day by day so that you can fail. And that is what is happening with you. No matter what you try to do it always results in failure. Children become vagabonds, they just keep going around in circles, nothing is happening. But that spell is going to be broken.

Today angels are going to be dispatched, wherever they put your name angels of the Lord God are going to remove it. Any altar that has been erected in your name it is going to be dismantled. Just like the statue of Dagan bowed down to the ark of God. Where they have put your name it is going to disappear in the name of Jesus.

Right now I take authority over every demonic altar that has been erected to hinder you, to keep you poor, to keep you sick, to hinder your children. I declare, angels thou are loosed. Go forth and remove their name, take away anything that belongs to them from the witches. Right now every demonic altar that has existed in your family, in your life, I command it to die by fire in the name of Jesus!

Balaam was the most powerful witch doctor in those times. Balak said, "I know that whoever you curse is cursed and whoever you bless is blessed."

So he sent his men with the fee for divination to go and summon Balaam.

Your enemies have paid so much money to see you fail but no matter what amount they paid, the blood of Jesus is going to prevail! I believe we are connected for a purpose and a reason. I believe as a matter of you reading this book demonic spells are being uprooted out of your life in Jesus Name.

Numbers 23:1-3 says,

Balaam said, "Build me seven altars here, and prepare seven bulls and seven rams for me." Balak did as Balaam said, and the two of them offered a bull and a ram on each altar. Then Balaam said to Balak, "Stay here beside your offering while I go aside. Perhaps the LORD will come to meet with me. Whatever he reveals to me I will tell you." Then he went off to a barren height.

Now, this offering was not being offered to God. It was being offered to the devil. But Balaam was a spiritual man; he could see what Balak could not see. He knew that there was another power behind the children of Israel. So he told Balak to stay while he goes aside. "**Perhaps the Lord will come to meet with me, whatever he reveals to me I will tell you. Then he went off to a barren height.**"

Balaam knew one thing: that God was walking around with the children of Israel in their camp.

So what Balaam did was make this offering to the devil to try and appease God, to make God jealous, that he might leave the children of Israel to come over and hear his request.

Verse 4 says,

God met with him, and Balaam said, "I have prepared seven altars, and on each altar I have offered a bull and a ram."

Balaam built up 7 altars, 7 is the number of completion. Your enemies have aimed to finish you completely, thinking that what they started will finish, and they have come with extra reinforcement, offering two sacrifices on each altar. But right now, every program that has been designed by the enemy in order to destroy you, I command it to be destroyed. I declare that it has a

BREAKING EVERY DEMONIC SPELL | 15

beginning and it has an end and today the hand of Jehovah is going to shame them in the name of Jesus.

Balaam knew where God was. He says I have prepared seven altars and on each altar I have offered a bull and a ram. He says are you interested in that God? He was trying to appease God so that He could tell him how to destroy the children of Israel.

That is what your enemies have been doing. They have been demanding, trying to find out how they can get you. But since you started going through deliverance there is a hedge of protection around you that they cannot understand. They are trying to find out how to destroy you but I declare permission denied. I declare there is a wall of fire around your family, your finances, your children, and your destiny in Jesus name!

And verse 5 says **The LORD put a word in Balaam's mouth and said, "Go back to Balak and give him this word.**'

God did not go to that altar. No, what he did is freeze Balaam's mouth, and put His words there. So when Balaam went back he could only speak what God says.

Verse 6 says,

> He went back to him and found him standing beside his offering, with all the Moabite officials. 7Then Balaam spoke his oracle: And Balaam said "Balak brought me from Aram, the king of Moab from the eastern mountains. 'Come,' he said, 'curse Jacob for me; come, denounce Israel.'
> How can I curse those whom God has not cursed? How can I denounce those whom the LORD has not denounced?

Right now whosoever has been planning to denounce you in the working place I declare it is not going to work. Whosoever is planning against you it shall not take place in the name of Jesus.

Today, there is a new anointing that is going to come upon you. That even the top witch doctors must consult God before they can touch you. And when they ask God for permission to destroy you, I hear this word ACCESS DENIED!

There is someone that has been trying to put another spell on your life but no more spells will work in your life in the name of Jesus. Every spell they have put over your finances is broken in the name of Jesus. Every curse of bad luck they have tried to put on your life I command it to be removed in the name of Jesus.

There is a spell that has been causing sickness in your family. There is a spell that had been released over your children, that's why their having trouble. But right now every spell over your children's photos; I break its powers in the name of Jesus. Every circle of sickness and diseases that have been going around your house I break its powers. Every spell over your children, I break its powers in the name of Jesus.

There has even been a spell of fear placed on your life. That is why sometimes you wake up in the middle of the night with nightmares and you don't know why. But right now every spell that has been put upon your house I command it to die by fire! You even have clothes you can never wear, you have a land you can never build, you have a place but you can't go there because every time you try there is fear that comes upon you. That is to show you there was a demonic sacrifice that was made where your life was concerned. But right now, that spell that has been cast over your life, over your finances, over your marriage, over your children, I command it to die by fire!

> God is not human, that he should lie, not a human being, that he should change his mind.
>
> (Numbers 23:19)

Somebody has been trying to change the mind of God where you're concerned. They've tried every way and failed, so they're trying to change the mind of God. But you are going to finish well in Jesus name.

Verse 20 says,

> I have received a command to bless; he has blessed, and I cannot change it.

Things are not going to change; your blessing is not going to change. That deliverance that began in your life is going to come to fulfillment. Your finances are coming through, that husband/wife is coming through, and those papers are coming through. There is no change of plans in the name of Jesus. That house is coming through, that career is coming through; your compensation is coming through in the name of Jesus.

Verse 21 says,

"No misfortune is seen in Jacob, no misery observed in Israel. The LORD their God is with them; the shout of the King is among them".

There shall be no misfortune in your life. Every bad luck every spell that has been causing failure over your life over your finances I break its powers, I command you to die by fire!

Num 4:9-10 Balaam says,

May those who bless you be blessed and those who curse you be cursed! Then Balak's anger burned against

Balaam. He struck his hands together and said to him, "I summoned you to curse my enemies, but you have blessed them these three times.

Balak came and complained that Balaam had blessed them instead of cursing them. Balak was forced to bless them instead of cursing them. God is going to turn every attempt to curse you into a blessing. When they go to the witch doctor it is going to backfire on them.

When you are under Gods protection, it doesn't matter how strong of a witch doctor they hire, the witch doctor will ask for God's permission and that permission has been denied! The next time they try they will hear "Don't mention this name again because whom God has blessed no man has cursed."

Below I have written 20 powerful prayer points for you to use to destroy every demonic spell that has been cast over your life. Pray them diligently, and I hear God say ACCESS DENIED when they try to curse you in the name of Jesus!

Break Every Demonic Spell

Before you pray, remember to put on the full armor of God according to Ephesians 6:10-18, touching each part of your body as you say it.

> *Repeat with me: "I put on the full armor of God. The helmet of salvation upon my head, the breastplate of righteousness in its place, the belt of truth around my waist, my feet shod with the readiness of the gospel of peace, taking the shield of faith in my left hand and the sword of the spirit in my right".*

In the Name of Jesus:

1. I take authority over all the powers, all the principalities, every ruler, and every evil spirit in high places. Satan the blood of Jesus is against you.

2. I take authority over every spell that has been cast over my life that has been causing failures; I break its powers in the name of Jesus! I command it to die by fire!

3. Every demonic council against my life that wants to activate a generational curse over my life I command it to die by fire!

4. Every demonic association over my life determining my fate I dismantle it in the name of Jesus!

5. Every council of witches that has been existing over my life I command it to die by fire!

6. I take authority over every demonic spell that has been controlling my life without knowing I bind it now and I command it to die by fire!

7. Every demonic spiritual sabotage that has been designed to destroy my finances, destroy my career, and destroy my destiny I bind it in the name of Jesus. I command it to die by fire!

8. Every demonic altar that has been raised up against my children, against my working place, against my business, against my marriage, against my finances, I command it to come down in the name of Jesus!

9. Right Now I take authority over every demonic spell that has been causing sickness and diseases over my life to die by fire!

10. I bind every demonic spell that has been causing failures in my relationship, I command it to die by fire!

11. Every spell that has been cast over my finances in order to cause failure I break its powers in the name of Jesus. I command it to die by fire!

12. Every spell that has been cast over my career in order to cause hindrance and delay I break its powers in the name of Jesus. I command it to die by fire!

13. Right now I take authority over every demonic spell that has been released over my projects to hinder me to die by fire!

14. I Take authority over every demonic spell that has been buried in the ground, in objects on my behalf in order to cause failure, I command it to die by fire!

15. Every spell that has been cast over my marriage and relationships in order to cause blockage I break its powers in the name of Jesus. I command it to die by fire!

16. Through the Blood of Jesus I cancel every demonic sacrifice that has been assigned to activate demonic spells over my life.

17. Every spell that has been cast over my health I command it to die by fire! Every sickness and diseases as a result of spells I break its powers in Jesus name!

What Can I Expect?

So now that you have your prayer points you need to understand that deliverance is not a onetime event but a process and you need to be consistent if you are going to destroy the enemies in your life. Let's look at a few things you can expect while going through your deliverance.

Firstly, expect to be set free and for peace to return back into your life. The Bible says that those who wait for the Lord shall not be ashamed. Also, start expecting God to give you a testimony, just like everyone else who has gone through our deliverance program.

There are some key steps you can follow to ensure you are doing everything properly in order to obtain your desired goals. (These are in addition to your daily prayer points listed in this book)

1. Locate the area of your need

According to what your situation may be, you need to identify the particular area or areas, which are most dire.

2. Find out what the Word of God says regarding that area

Select the appropriate scriptures promising you what you desire and meditate upon them. Write them on your walls where you can see them. Even if it means writing it on yourself so you won't forget to recite them during the day. Do whatever it takes but make sure you are replaying them in your mind daily.

3. Exercise one of the following prayers while expecting your deliverance

· 3 day Night Vigil at the Sanctuary (i.e. praying and confessing the Word from 10 pm to 5 am for 3 nights in a row)

· 3 Day Fast (i.e. praying, fasting, and confessing the Word daily from 6 am to 6 pm for 3 days. Alternatively you can fast straight through the 3 days only breaking for communion)

· 3-Day Fast Prayer Vigil at the Sanctuary (i.e. praying, fasting, and confessing the Word daily from 10 am to 6 pm for 3 days. Again you can fast continually for 3 days apart from communion)

· 3 + Days Dry Fast (i.e. praying, fasting, and confessing the Word for 3 or more days without taking food or drink). Please note: This should only be done under pastoral recommendation.

4. Pray aggressively while believing that you receive your deliverance

Hebrews 11:6 says, *"We must believe that He is and that He is a rewarder of them that diligently seek Him".*

5. Make any adjustments in your life and repent as the Holy Spirit leads

You have to make sure that you are not leaving any open doors for the enemy to regain access in your life.

6. This is the most crucial step. You must sow your seed to seal your deliverance

Most people sow consecutive seeds, giving it the same name according to their expectation from God regarding their deliverance. To truly succeed in spiritual warfare you have to be a sower. The Bible says in Deut 16:16 to "never appear before God empty handed". So as you are expecting to receive something from God you need to be giving back something to Him as well.

7. Lastly, prepare yourself for your miracle physically and spiritually

Be vigorous in attending service as much as possible in order to receive the ministration of the Word and the laying on of the hands by the man of God. Also, attend your deliverance sessions regularly if you have been assigned to a mentor.

Bishop Climate Ministries
P.O. Box 67884, London, SE5 9JJ
England, United Kingdom
Tel: +44 7984 115900
Email: partners@bishopclimate.org

Yes Bishop! I want to come into agreement with you that as I sow my seed of Deliverance according to the number of my Age, I believe every spell is broken and destroyed in the name of Jesus!

£ _____

Here is my Prayer request covering the 7 areas I desire the Lord to manifest His Miracles in my life:

_____

_____

_____

_____

_____

_____

_____

_____

_____

(Continued on Back)

Name:

_____

Address:

_____

_____

_____

Telephone:

_____

Email:

_____

NOTE: You can also sow your special seed SAFELY & SECURELY online via www.bishopclimate.org

Bishop Climate Ministries is the Healing & Deliverance Ministry founded by Bishop Climate under the anointing and direction of the Holy Spirit. God has anointed Bishop Climate with incredible power to set the captives free. Many people who were unable to get deliverance anywhere else find their freedom as they attend special deliverance sessions conducted through this ministry. The vision of Bishop Climate Ministries is to reach over 1 billion people with the message of deliverance and prosperity, especially in understanding the things of the spirit. Many people are bound because of lack of knowledge and one of the goals of this ministry is to set people free through education.

Child of God I want you to know how much I appreciate you and how special you are to me. That is why God keeps giving me the wisdom to write these books at such a time as this. He sees your heart and wants you to experience the abundant life that Jesus died for. And so do I. Your support for our ministry is crucial and I hope that you will always continue to lift us up in prayer to God.

I want to take this opportunity to encourage you to partner with us at Bishop Climate Ministries. Hundreds have testified of the miracles that have taken place in their life just as a result of sowing into this ministry and I want you to be able to experience that 100 fold return Jesus spoke about regarding sowing seed into good ground. The Bible says in Proverbs 11:24 *"One person gives freely, yet gains even more; another withholds unduly, but comes to poverty"*. Your prayers and financial support are crucial to take this message of salvation and deliverance around the world. And as you do that you can be sure that God is going to bless you beyond your wildest imaginations. There is a 4-fold anointing that you step under when you become a partner with Bishop Climate Ministries. It is the anointing that God has put over my life and this ministry according to Isaiah 11:2. That is the anointing of Divine Direction, Divine Connections, Divine Provision and Divine Protection.

Please understand how much I value you. Your support for our ministry is so crucial and your prayers are as a pillar to us. Your partnership with this ministry is so important and that's why we are committed to praying for you daily and lifting your needs up before God. When you send in your donation please send me a prayer request as well so I can intercede on your behalf before God. I look forward to seeing you in person at our Healing and Deliverance Centre in London, England or at one of our Healing and Deliverance Miracle Crusades.

Remember this is the Ministry where the captives are set free and souls are refreshed.

Remain blessed,

Bishop Climate Irungu

Victory Over The Spirit Of Humiliation & Oppression

Breaking The Curse Of

Good Beginnings & Bad Endings

Victory Over Demonic Assignments

Overcoming Every Generational Hatred

Overcoming Persistent Enemies

Destroying Every Demonic Blockage

Victory Over Every Troubling Spirit

Destroying Every Spirit of Poverty & Lack

Destroying Every Demonic Covenant Over Your Life

Victory Over Every Appointment With Death

Binding the Strongman

Uprooting Every Demonic Prophecy

Victory Over Every Evil Wish

Uprooting Every Territorial Sorcerers

Victory Over Demonic Storms (Marine Spirit)

Bringing Down Goliath (Spirit of Fear)

Dealing With the Spirit of Disappointment

Victory Over The Lying Spirit

Casting Out The Spirit of Anger

Breaking The Spirit Of Pride

Destroying Every Demonic Contamination

Burning Every Spirit Of Mockery

Order Enquiries: Please call our offices or order online at www.bishopclimate.me

Printed in Great Britain
by Amazon